Ama suwa, Ama quella, Ama llulla
Do not steal, do not be idle, and do not lie.

The three golden rules of the Inca
Empire of the Sun

www.rourkepublishing.com

Editor: Frank Sloan

Munay and The Magic Lake is based
on an Inca tale from Ecuador
included in *Latin American Folktales*
by Genevieve Barlow, 1966

To Shayda, my own Munay
    -S.S

Library of Congress Cataloging-in-Publication Data

Sepehri, Sandy.
    Munay and the magic lake : based on an Inca tale / retold by Sandy
Sepehri ; illustrated by Brian Demeter.
      p. cm. -- (Latin American tales and myths)
    ISBN 1-60044-146-7
    1. Incas--Folklore. 2. Inca mythology. 3. Central America--Folklore.
4. South America--Folklore.   I. Demeter, Brian, ill. II. Title.
III. Series.
F3429.3.F6S48 2007
398.2'08998323--dc22
                                            2006014933

Printed in the USA

Latin American Tales
and Myths

MUNAY
AND THE
MAGIC LAKE

Based On An Inca Tale

Retold by Sandy Sepehri
Illustrated by Brian Demeter
Cover design and storyboards
by Nicola Stratford
Project Consultant: Silvina Peralta Ramos

Rourke
Publishing LLC
Vero Beach, Florida 32964

With all his riches and all his power, the greatest ruler of **Peru**, the **Sapa Inca**, was the saddest man on Earth. His only child, a boy of twelve years, was deathly ill.

On the softest mattress, stuffed with the wool from the **vicuña**, the young prince would toss and turn, burning from fever and barely able to eat.

"Neither gold nor my authority can bring my beloved son back to health!" cried the Sapa Inca one night. He prayed to **Viracocha**, the sun god. "Please help my son!"

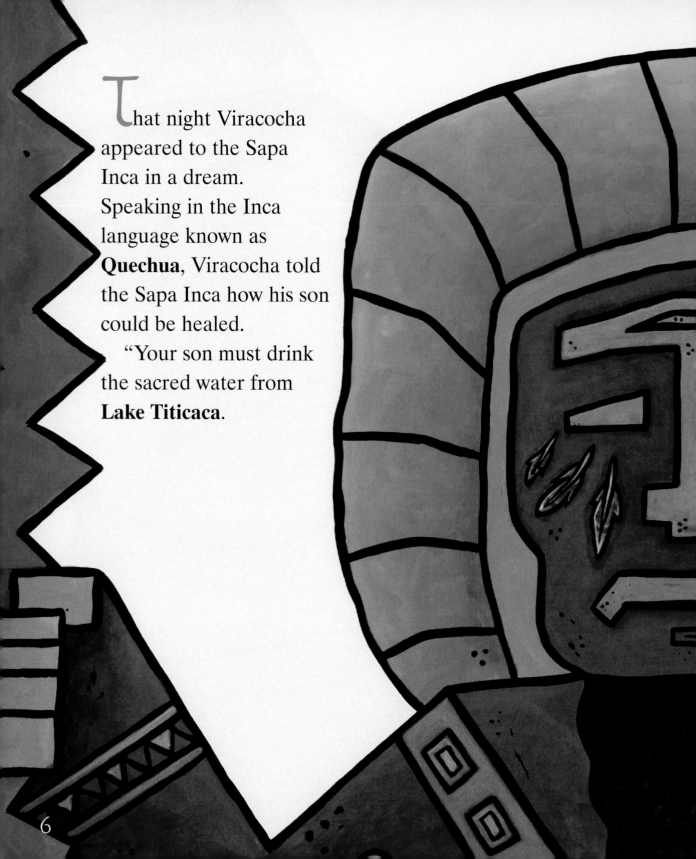

That night Viracocha appeared to the Sapa Inca in a dream. Speaking in the Inca language known as **Quechua**, Viracocha told the Sapa Inca how his son could be healed.

"Your son must drink the sacred water from **Lake Titicaca**.

6

This magical lake is at the end of the world, where the water meets the sky and is guarded by three fierce creatures. Only one who is pure of heart will be allowed to bring back the water. I will send my servant sparrows to help in this mission."

Two brothers, Tumi and Guano, begged their parents to allow them to seek the magic lake. They said that they wanted to help the prince get well when in fact they were only interested in escaping from their chores.

Their young sister, **Munay**, begged to go on the journey. She was the only one who truly wanted to help save the prince. But their parents would only let the two brothers go. So, the brothers set out to find the magic lake.

Being lazy, it didn't take them long to tire of their journey. After only two hours of walking, they sat under some trees to eat their dinner of toasted corn kernels. Just then, a group of six sparrows flew down and stood on the ground in front of the brothers.

The leader of the sparrows said to the boys, "We are the servants of Viracocha."

"You are a flock of dirty beggars coming to take our food. Be gone!"

And the insulted sparrows flew away.

"How much further is it to the lake?" asked Tumi. Guano grumbled. "Too far. Let us fill the jar with water from any lake."

And that is exactly what they did.

When they arrived with their jar of water, the Sapa Inca desperately grabbed it and brought it to his son's lips. The brothers exchanged nervous glances, realizing that the Sapa Inca was trying to heal his son, before rewarding them.

The frail young prince sat up and obediently drank from the jar. Suddenly his whole body began to shake from fever and he sputtered the words, "No more!"

The Sapa Inca began to wonder about the water. "How was your journey to the magic lake?" he asked the boys. "Was it difficult collecting the water?"

"We faced no difficulty at all," Tumi answered.

At this, the Sapa Inca knew the brothers were lying. He had them jailed and vowed they would never be released.

The news of the brothers quickly spread throughout the village. When Munay heard, she begged her parents to let her go find the magic lake.

"Perhaps if I bring back the healing water, the Sapa Inca will set the boys free."

So her parents agreed, and Munay set out bravely on her mission.

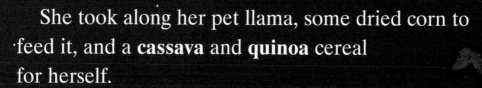

She took along her pet llama, some dried corn to
feed it, and a **cassava** and **quinoa** cereal
for herself.

The first night she slept, snug and warm against
her llama, in the shelter of some large rocks.
But, when she heard the hungry cry of the puma,
she feared for her pet and sent him home.

The next night Munay slept in the branches of a tall tree. When she awoke, she saw six sparrows talking among themselves.

She offered them some food. "Please take this corn, along with my gratitude." The sparrows were impressed with the corn and with Munay's good manners.

Munay told them she would bring back water to heal the prince.

"Ah," said the sparrows in unison. "We are the servants of Viracocha. We shall help you."

Then each sparrow lifted a wing and revealed a shining feather. "Take these six feathers. Shape them into a fan and they will fly you to the lake. But beware of the three fierce creatures that guard the lake."

Holding the beautiful fan in her hands, Munay whispered, "Take me to the magic lake."

A gentle breeze began to blow and Munay was lifted into the sky. She held onto the fan and smiled with surprise at the sight of the trees beneath her, blurring into a giant green streak.

Within minutes, she landed softly on the ground. In front of her she could see a bright blue lake, rising up to meet the sky.

Suddenly she heard a great flapping sound. She looked up, and to her horror she saw a flying serpent. This must be the first fierce creature.

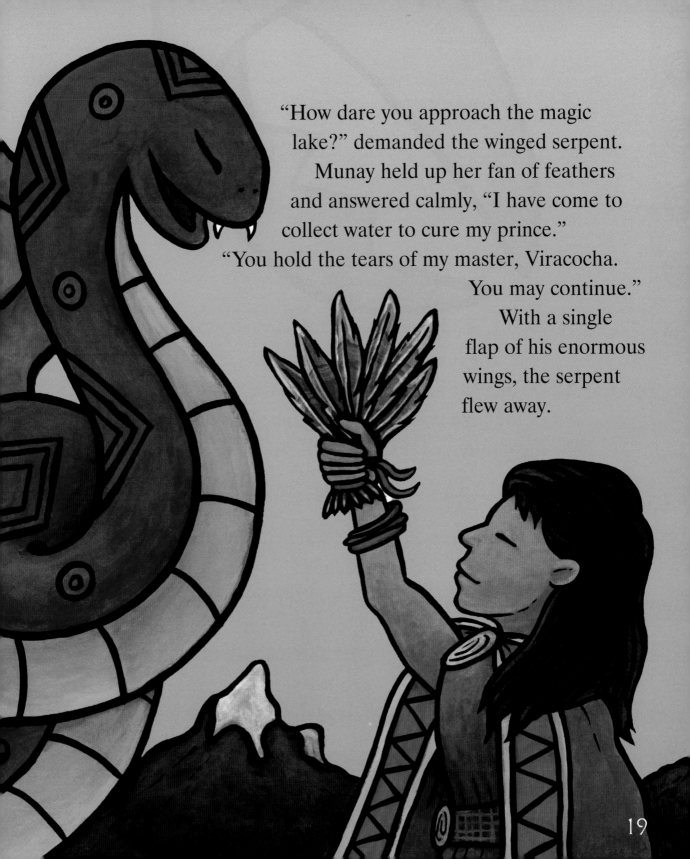

"How dare you approach the magic
lake?" demanded the winged serpent.
Munay held up her fan of feathers
and answered calmly, "I have come to
collect water to cure my prince."
"You hold the tears of my master, Viracocha.
You may continue."
With a single
flap of his enormous
wings, the serpent
flew away.

19

Munay walked bravely on toward the lake. As she did, she saw a giant hole in the sand. From out of the hole crawled a huge crab. This had to be the second fierce creature.

"What business do you have at this lake?" asked the crab.

"I am here to collect water to heal the prince," Munay said, displaying her fan.

The crab got a closer look at the feathers and saw that they were indeed the tears of Viracocha.

The crab did not say another word but scrambled back down his hole.

21

As soon as she was alone, Munay picked up her jar, filled it with water, and asked the fan to fly her back to the Sapa Inca.

For the final time, she was flown through the air and delivered softly in front of the palace.

"I wish to see the Sapa Inca," she told the guards, and was taken to the prince's room, where she found the Sapa Inca pacing back and forth and the prince lying still on his bed.

"I bring water from the magic lake to cure the prince," Munay boldly announced.

Afraid that she might be lying, the Sapa Inca asked her how her journey had been.

"Very frightening. There were three terrible creatures guarding the lake. One was a flying serpent, the second was a giant crab, and the third was an alligator who wanted to eat me."

"How did you escape these creatures, my child," asked the Sapa Inca

Munay pulled out the feathers and spread them into a fan. "With these."

When he recognized the teardrops of Viracocha, the Sapa Inca cried tears of his own. So he took Munay's jar and brought it to his son's lips. The prince swallowed a small sip of the water. Slowly his eyes began to open and his cheeks filled with color. Seeing his father for the first time since he fell into a fever, the young prince smiled.

Overcome with joy, the Sapa Inca turned to Munay. "Dear child, ask what you want and it shall be yours."

"Thank you," said Munay. "I want only three things. First, for your son to return to full health; second, for my brothers to be released from jail; and third, for the safe return of these feathers."

She untied the feathers from the fan, and the feathers flew out of the window.

Amazed, the prince said to his father, "Please free the girl's brothers."

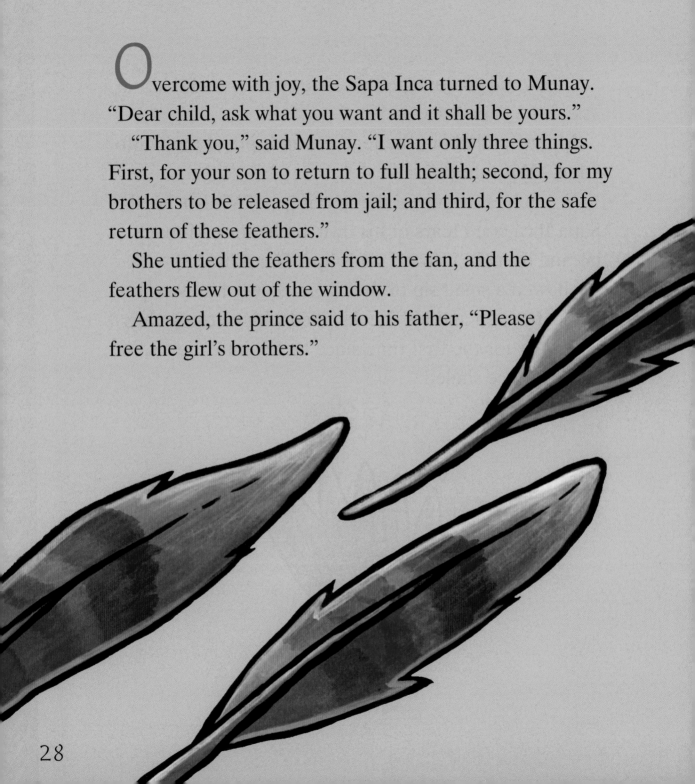

"It shall be done," replied the Sapa Inca. And you
must come here and live at the palace."

"I cannot leave my parents, who are very good to me."

"I see that you already know the lesson it has taken
me a lifetime to learn: the only real wealth in this world
is the people you love."

The Sapa Inca released Tumi and Guano, and they
were led into the room.

"Let us go home, my brothers," Munay said. On the way, she spoke. "I am sorry you have no treasure to bring back with you, my brothers."

Tumi and Guano had changed because of their stay in prison.

"Munay, you are wrong. We are bringing home the greatest treasure of all—you!"

And the three children walked home, feeling like the wealthiest people on Earth.

GLOSSARY

cassava (cah SAH vah) – a plant, with a starchy, edible root

Lake Titicaca (LAYK Titty CAH cah) – second largest lake in South America, in the Andes Mountains, with Peru to the west and Bolivia to the east. *Titicaca* has been translated as Rock of the Puma or Crag of Lead.

Munay (moo NAY) – an Inca word for love and compassion

Peru (purr EW) – the third largest country in South America, just south of the equator, and home to the remains of the Inca Empire

Quechua (KECH wua) – a universal language, amongst Inca tribes

quinoa (quin OH ah) – a type of pigweed that produces a small grain that Incas ground into a cereal

Sapa Inca (sa PAH INK ah) – an Inca emperor

vicuña (vich OO niah) – an animal, related to the camel, sheared for its fine-quality wool

Viracocha (veer ah COACH ah) – the Inca sun god, who rose from Lake Titicaca, represented with sun rays shooting from his face, the sun for a crown, thunderbolts in his hands and tears descending from his eyes as rain

ABOUT THE AUTHOR

Sandy Sepehri lives with her husband, Shahram, and their three children in Florida. She has a bachelor's degree and writes freelance articles and children's stories.